Ami Ami Dogs

SERIOUSLY CUTE CROCHET!

BY MITSUKI HOSHI

HARPER DESIGN

An Imprint of HarperCollins Publishers

AMI AMI DOGS
Copyright © Mitsuki Hoshi 2008
Original Japanese language edition published by Bunka Publishing Bureau.
English translation rights arranged with Bunka Publishing Bureau., Tokyo
through Nippon Shuppan Hanbai Inc.

First published in 2011 by:
Harper Design
An Imprint of HarperCollins*Publishers*
10 East 53rd Street
New York, NY 10022
Tel.: (212) 207-7000
Fax: (212) 207-7654
harperdesign@harpercollins.com
www.harpercollins.com

Distributed throughout the world by:
HarperCollins*Publishers*
10 East 53rd Street, New York, NY 10022
Fax: (212) 207-7654

HarperCollins books may be purchased for educational,
business, or sales promotional use. For information, please write:
Special Markets Department, HarperCollins Publishers,
10 East 53rd Street, New York, NY 10022.

Book Design: Tomoko Okayama, Andrew Pothecary
Cover Design: Andrew Pothecary
Photography: Yasuo Nagumo
Line Drawing: day studio (Satomi Dairaku)
Editorial Cooperation: Shingo Taneda
English translation: Seishi Maruyama
Copy-editing: Alma Reyes
Chief Editor and Production: Rico Komanoya (ricorico)

Library of Congress Control Number: 2010935073
ISBN: 9780062025708

Printed in China

Pictured on previous page:
Miniature Dachshund (See page 54.)
Dog house, food bowl, and dog food (See page 70.)

Contents

Chihuahua

(See page 46.)

Welsh Corgi

(See page 48.)

Left: fawn
Right: tricolor

Japanese Shiba

(See page 32.)

Cavalier King Charles Spaniel

(See page 50.)

Left: tricolor
Right: Blenheim

Miniature Dachshund

(See page 54.)

From left clockwise: red, cream,
black and tan, chocolate and cream

Siberian Husky

(See page 56.)

Labrador Retriever

(See page 53.)

Maltese

(See page 58.)

Miniature Schnauzer

(See page 62.)

French Bulldog

(See page 64.)

Beagle

(See pages 59 and 60.)

Pug

(See page 66.)

Cellular Phone Accessories

(See page 68.)

Basic Knitting Techniques

Basically the same sewing method is used for all the crocheted dogs in this book. If you can knit a Japanese Shiba, you can use the same technique for the other types of dogs, as well. All you have to do is change the color of the thread, as instructed, while referring to the pattern for each dog.

As seen in the photo below, the three dogs are crocheted in the same way, but you can make them look different by using threads in different thicknesses. From the left, the heights of the sitting dogs, from head to toe, are: approximately 2 inches, 3 inches, and 5 inches, respectively. The Japanese Shiba shown on page 3 of the Contents page is medium-sized, or about 3 inches tall. You may use this as a reference for the sizes of the dogs.

The crocheting method is the same for the large, medium, and small dogs. Rows should be started with highest row number.

Materials (medium-sized Japanese Shiba)

Body Brown and white bulky thread
Synthetic cotton
Eyes Black plastic sewing buttons,
　2 pieces, 0.24 in
Nose Black nose round button,
　1 piece, 0.47 in
(See page 32 for details.)

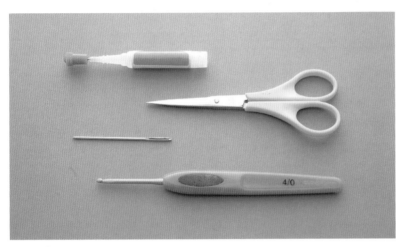

Tools

Crochet hook No. 4/0
Wool needle
Scissors
Glue

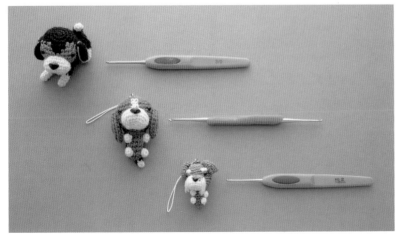

Thickness of threads and crochet hooks

Small dog (height: approx. 2.36 in) =
light thread, crochet hook No. 3/0

Medium dog strap (height: approx. 2.17 in) =
light thread, crochet hook No. 3/0 or 2/0

Small dog strap (height: approx.1.38 in) =
fine thread, crochet hook No. 2/0

Japanese Shiba   See pages 8 and 30.

The crocheting method is the same for the large, medium, and small dogs. Rows should be started with highest row number.

Materials

[Large dog]
Beige thread, 0.81 oz; white thread, 0.42 oz
Synthetic cotton
Black plastic sewing buttons, 2 pieces, 0.31 in
Black nose round button, 1 piece, 0.59 in

[Medium dog]
Brown bulky thread, 0.6 oz;
  white bulky thread, 0.28 oz
Synthetic cotton
Black plastic sewing buttons, 2 pieces, 0.24 in
Black nose round button, 1 piece, 0.47 in

[Small dog]
Brown light thread, 0.18 oz;
  white light thread, 0.14 oz
Synthetic cotton
Black plastic sewing buttons, 2 pieces, 0.16 in
Black nose round button, 1 piece, 0.35 in

Tools

Large dog: crochet hook No. 6/0
Medium dog: crochet hook No. 4/0
Small dog: crochet hook No. 3/0

Step-by-step method

1. Crochet each body part.
2. Stuff cotton inside the head, body, and legs.
3. Attach the eyes and eyebrows on the head.
4. Attach the nose on the mouth, and stuff cotton in it.
5. Attach the mouth to the head by rolled darning.
6. Attach the body to the head by rolled darning.
7. Attach the legs to the body by rolled darning.
8. Attach the ears to the head, and the tail to the body by rolled darning.

Head   c=center

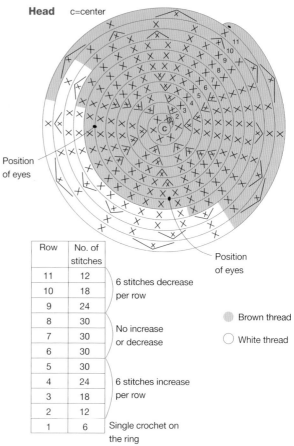

Position of eyes

Position of eyes

Row	No. of stitches	
11	12	6 stitches decrease per row
10	18	
9	24	
8	30	No increase or decrease
7	30	
6	30	
5	30	
4	24	6 stitches increase per row
3	18	
2	12	
1	6	Single crochet on the ring

◍ Brown thread

○ White thread

Mouth

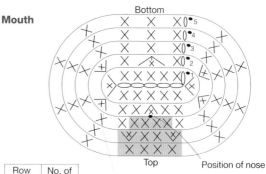

Bottom

Top   Position of nose

Row	No. of stitches	
5	15	No increase or decrease
4	15	2 stitches decrease
3	17	No increase or decrease
2	17	3 stitches increase
1	14	Single crochet on five chain stitches

(See page 45 for the chart symbols.)

Body

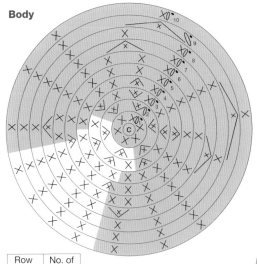

Row	No. of stitches	
10	12	No increase or decrease
9	12	2 stitches decrease
8	14	No increase or decrease
7	14	4 stitches decrease
6	18	No increase or decrease
5	18	2 stitches increase
4	16	2 stitches decrease
3	18	6 stitches increase per row
2	12	
1	6	Single crochet on the ring

Ears

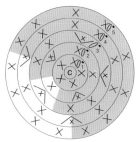

2 pieces

Row	No. of stitches	
5	12	No increase or decrease
4	12	2 stitches increase
3	10	3 stitches increase
2	7	2 stitches increase
1	5	Single crochet on the ring

Legs

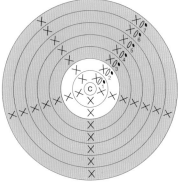

Front legs, 2 pieces

Row	No. of stitches	
7	5	No increase or decrease
6~3	5 each	
2	5	
1	5	Single crochet on the ring

Hind legs, 2 pieces

Row	No. of stitches	
6	5	No increase or decrease
5~3	5 each	
2	5	
1	5	Single crochet on the ring

Tail

Row	No. of stitches	
2	5	Single crochet on 6 chain stitches
1	6	

Position of body parts

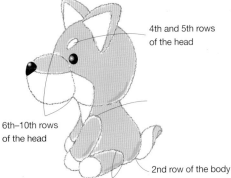

2nd–5th rows of the head

4th and 5th rows of the head

6th–10th rows of the head

2nd row of the body

2nd–4th rows of the body

Knitting the head

Making a slipknot for the central ring

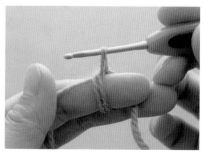

1 To make a slipknot for the central ring, wind the thread twice around your index finger.

2 Hold the end of the thread with your index finger and middle finger, and insert the crochet hook into the ring to pull the thread on the left end.

3 Pull the hook through the ring to tighten the ring around your finger.

Making chain stitches in the center

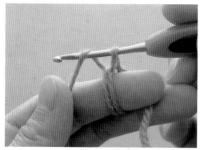

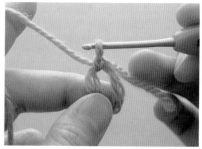

1 Hook the thread and pull it through the ring once again.

2 The chain stitch is completed in the center.

3 Once the chain stitch is completed in the center, pull your index finger out of the ring and hook your index finger on the thread you are going to work on. It is easier to crochet if you hold the thread with your ring finger and pinky finger.

Making single crochets (first row)

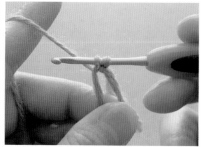

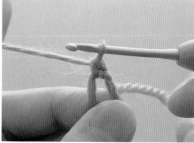

1 Insert the crochet hook into the ring and hook the thread.

2 Insert the hooked thread into the ring and then pull it out. Hook the thread once again, and pull out the two stitches together.

3 After pulling out the thread, the single crochet is completed.

4 Insert the crochet hook into the ring, as previously done, and hook the thread.

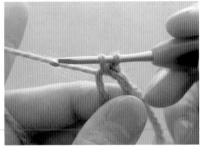

5 Insert the thread into the ring and pull it out.

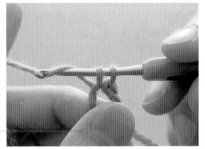

6 Hook the thread with the crochet hook to pull it through the two stitches.

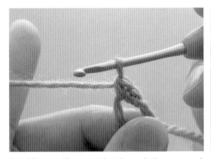

7 After pulling out the thread, the second stitch of a single crochet is completed.

8 Repeat the same steps, and make six stitches with a single crochet.

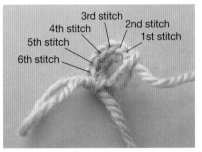

9 When six stitches are completed, loosen the ring with the hook to pull it out.

Tightening the ring

1 First, pull the end of the thread in the center, and pull the ring that is tugged while tightening the ring.

2 Once the ring is tightened, pull the end of the thread in the center to tighten the other ring.

3 When the ring is tightened, the first row is completed. Tighten the ring and insert the crochet hook.

Sewing without starting chains in the center (2nd row)

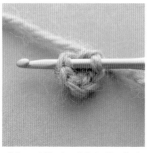

Sewing two stitches

1 Insert the hook into the first stitch with a single crochet.

2 Pass the hook into the thread as shown in steps 4 to 6 for the first row, and pull it out through the ring to make a single crochet.

3 The first stitch of the second row is completed.

1 For the 2nd row, sew two single crochets into each of the six stitches of the first row to increase six stitches, making twelve stitches in total in the 2nd row. (See page 32.)

Changing threads

1 From the 3rd row, continue to crochet in circles until the 5th row. (See page 32.) Then, from the 6th row, sew without increasing the number of stitches until the 8th row. Change the thread in the middle of the 8th row.

2 Insert the hook into the 10th stitch of the 8th row, and pull the thread out.

3 Loop the different-colored thread around your finger and hook it. Change threads in the middle of the previous stitch.

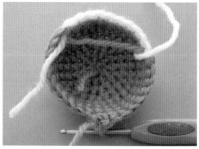

4 Pull the needle with the two stitches hooked together, and sew single crochets.

5 On the 10th stitch using the white thread, hang the brown thread looped over your finger, then pull it through as you did in steps 3 and 4 to change threads.

6 The photo above shows the thread crossing on the reverse side. Be careful not to tighten the crossing thread too much, because the stitch on the right side will be puckered.

Making a single decrease

1 From the 9th row, make a single decrease to decrease the stitches. First, insert the hook into a stitch to grab the thread.

2 Pull out the hooked thread.

3 Insert the hook into the next stitch, and hook the thread to pull it out. Here, three stitches are hooked on the crochet hook.

4 Pull out the three stitches together. This makes a single decrease with a single crochet.

5 Referring to the pattern on page 32, repeat a single decrease and a single crochet alternately to decrease the number of stitches.

6 Sewing stage until the 11th row

Making a slip stitch

1 To finish with a slip stitch, insert the hook into the next stitch and pull out the thread.

2 Pull out the other thread hooked on the crochet hook on the left side.

3 Pull out the thread through the ring and cut the thread.

4 Pull the thread to tighten it.

Making a mouth

Making chain stitches

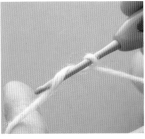 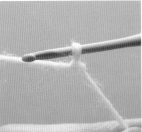 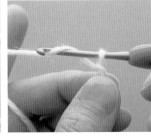 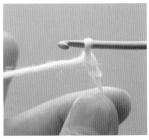

1 Loop the thread on the hook from the other side to your side, then twist the hook from your side to the other side. Hook the thread to pull it through.

2 The thread is pulled out.

3 Hook the thread to pull it through.

4 A chain stitch is completed.

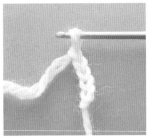 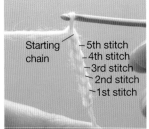  

Making a single crochet

5 Repeat steps 3 and 4 to make five chain stitches.

6 Then, make a starting chain.

Starting chain — 5th stitch
— 4th stitch
— 3rd stitch
— 2nd stitch
— 1st stitch

1 Sew single crochets on the chain stitches. Insert the hook to pull the top of the chain stitch of the 5th stitch on the reverse side.

2 Pull out the hooked thread.

 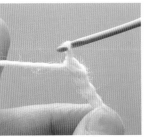 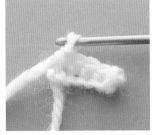 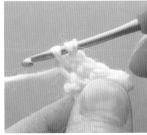

3 Hook the thread to pull the two stitches together.

4 The thread is pulled out, and a single crochet is sewn into the chain stitch.

5 Repeating the same steps, sew four more single crochets into the top of the chain stitches on the reverse side.

6 At the end of the row, increase a stitch by sewing two single crochets into one stitch. (See page 71.)

7 Two stitches are sewn. Now work on the other side, too.

8 When you complete one row, sew two single crochets at the end of the row.

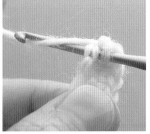

1 Insert the hook into the 1st stitch of the 1st row and pull out the thread.

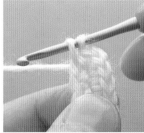

2 Hook the thread on the left to pull it out.

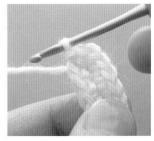

3 A slip stitch is finished, and the 1st row is completed.

Sewing the 2nd Row

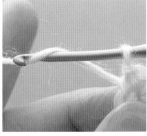

1 First, make a starting chain on the 2nd row.

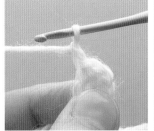

2 A starting chain is completed.

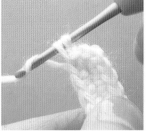

3 Then, make a single crochet.

Making a double decrease

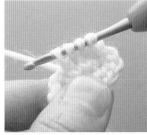

1 Insert the needle into the three stitches, then pull out the thread to hook it. The hook is holding four stitches.

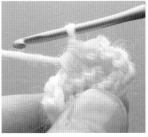

2 Pull the four stitches through together at once. This makes a double decrease with a single crochet. (See page 71.)

Making the 3rd row

1 Change the thread in the middle of the 3rd row.

2 Sew five rows to complete the mouth.

Making the tail

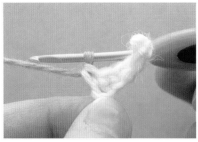  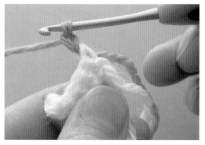

1 Sew six chain stitches and a starting chain, then make six single crochets as you did for the mouth. Change threads when pulling out the last stitch.

2 Make a starting chain in the 2nd row.

3 Turn over the work and start sewing single crochets on the reverse side.

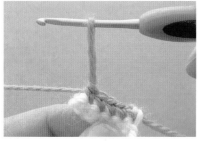 

4 After sewing five single crochets, pull out the thread through the ring and cut it.

5 The tail is completed.

Working with the thread's end

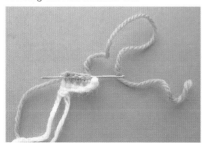 

1 Pass the thread that you pulled out into the wool needle, then pass it through the stitches before cutting the thread's end.

2 Leave the thread without cutting it.

Making the body, legs, and ears

To make the body, legs, and ears, make a slipknot in the center as shown on pages 34 and 35. Sew single crochets, then make a slip stitch as shown on page 39. From the 2nd row, make a starting chain, then sew single crochets as shown in steps 1 to 3 on page 39.

Completed parts

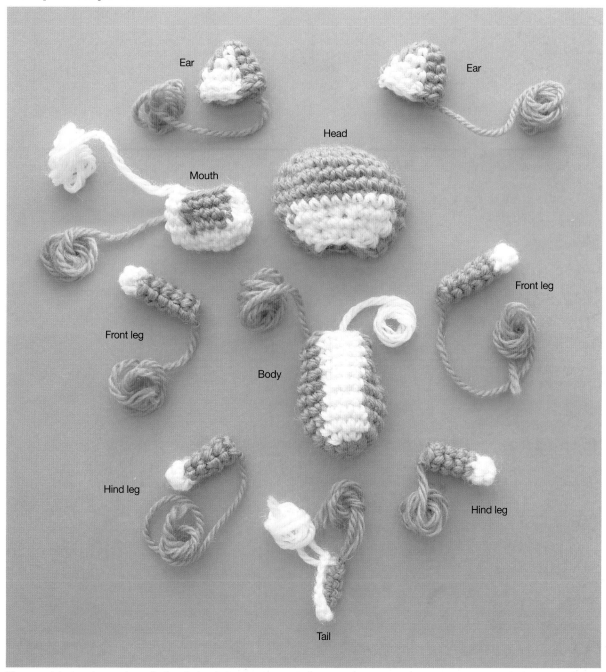

The completed parts are shown in the photo above.
Leave the thread ends long for the finishing stage.

Stuffing cotton

Stuff cotton into the head and the body.

A toothpick may be handy for stuffing cotton into the legs and other small parts.

Making the head

Attaching the eyes

1 Pass white thread through the wool needle, and pass the needle from the back through the eyes. Make a knot at the end of the thread.

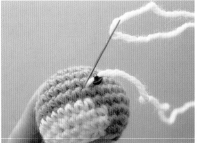

2 Pass the needle back through where you pulled it out, and pass it through the position of the other eye.

3 Attach the other eye in the same way, and pull the needle through the rear side.

Attaching the eyebrows

1 To attach the eyebrows, continue using the same thread you used for attaching the eyes. Pull the needle through the rear side, and pass it through the position of the eyebrow. Sew three straight stitches.

2 Continue sewing, and pass the needle through the position of the other eyebrow.

3 Sew three straight stitches, then pull the needle through the bottom side.

4 Pass the thread one more time from the front through the back, and cut it with scissors while pulling it. In this way, the thread is kept inside and is prevented from being pulled out.

5 The head, with eyes and eyebrows, is done.

1 Apply glue on the stem of the nose, and push it into the mouth.

Attaching the mouth

2 On the row of the mouth where the thread colors change, attach the triangular nose so its angle is pointing down. Glue the nose, then stuff cotton into the mouth.

1 Pass the thread's end through the wool needle. Attach the head by rolled darning.

2 The head and mouth are complete.

Attaching the parts

Attaching the body

Attaching the legs

Attaching the ears and tail

As in the previous steps, attach the body to the head by rolled darning.

Attach the front and hind legs to the body.

Attach the ears and tail to complete the work.

Various types and sizes of eyes and noses

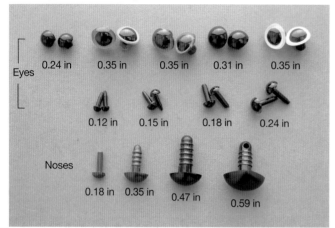

Eyes

0.24 in 0.35 in 0.35 in 0.31 in 0.35 in

0.12 in 0.15 in 0.18 in 0.24 in

Noses

0.18 in 0.35 in 0.47 in 0.59 in

If you wish to outline the rims of the eyes, paint the reverse side of the eyes with a whiteout pen.

There are various types and sizes of eyes (0.12–0.35 in) and noses (0.18–0.59 in). Black plastic sewing buttons are used for black eyes of 0.24 in and 0.31 in sizes. For other colored eyes, the eyes and noses of stuffed animals can also be used.

Weights

If you are making a seated dog, stuff some heavy weights, such as pellets or nuts, with cotton in the base of the dog to stabilize the dog's weight.

For beginners of sewing knitted dogs

Crochet chart symbols

Each knitting method for every dog is accompanied by charts. Refer to the chart symbols below, and start from the first row. The knitting method is explained in the steps for the Japanese Shiba (pages 32–43) in addition to the instructions on page 71.

 Chain stitch

 Single crochet

 Single increase with a single crochet

 Single decrease with a single crochet

 Double decrease with a single crochet

Slip stitch

Ridge stitch

Materials

The Japanese Shiba shown in this book are all medium-sized, except for the large dog on the right side in the photo on page 30, and the small dog straps shown on pages 28–29.
The types of yarns used for each work are also indicated, but you can freely use various yarns in different thicknesses to make dogs in different sizes.

Tools

Only crochet hooks in different sizes are specified in the step-by-step method for each dog. You will also need a wool needle, scissors, and glue for all the works. See page 31.

Step-by-step method

Refer to the procedures in the step-by-step method for the Japanese Shiba. However, you can freely change the order of attaching the ears, legs, tails, and other parts. You can also adjust the positions of attaching each part according to your preference, as long as you check the overall balance.

Knitting the head

The dog's head is knitted in a circle without making a starting chain, continuing from one row to the other. This is called "circular knitting." You might lose track of the number of rows that you have completed. To avoid this, it may be convenient to insert a piece of thread in a different color as a marker at the beginning of the second row. You can also use row counting rings to count the number of rows easily.

Chihuahua   See page 4.

Use the same plain-colored thread
used in the Japanese Shiba for the
seated dog's body and legs.

Materials

White mohair thread, 1 roll
  Standing dog: 0.52 oz
  Seated dog: 0.49 oz
Synthetic cotton
Black plastic sewing buttons, 2 pairs,
  0.31 in
Black nose round buttons, 2 pieces,
  0.47 in
Crochet hook No. 4/0

Step-by-step method

Standing dog:
1. Sew each body part.
2. Stuff cotton inside the head, body,
   and legs.
3. Attach eyes on the head.
4. Attach the nose on the mouth and
   stuff cotton in it.
5. Attach the mouth to the head by
   rolled darning.
6. Sew the last row of the body with the
   remaining thread, tie and knot.
7. Sew the last row of the head with the
   remaining thread, tie lightly, and sew the
   body by rolled darning.
8. Attach the legs to the body by rolled
   darning.
9. Attach the ears to the head and the tail
   to the body by rolled darning.

Seated dog:
1–5. Same as above.
6. Sew the last row of the head with the
   remaining thread, tie and knot, then
   sew the body to the side of the head by
   rolled darning.
7. Follow steps 8 and 9 above.

Head   c=center

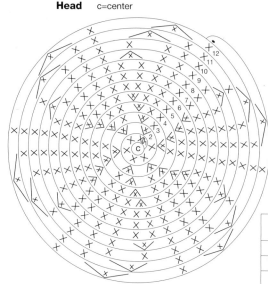

Row	No. of stitches	
12	12	6 stitches decrease per row
11	18	
10	24	No increase or decrease
9	24	6 stitches decrease
8	30	No increase or decrease
7	30	
6	30	
5	30	6 stitches increase per row
4	24	
3	18	
2	12	
1	6	Single crochet on the center of the ring

Body of standing dog

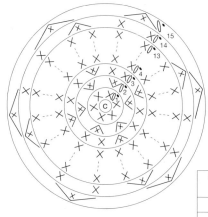

Row	No. of stitches	
15	6	6 stitches decrease
14	12	4 stitches decrease
13	16	No increase or decrease
12~5	16 each	
4	16	
3	16	4 stitches increase
2	12	6 stitches increase
1	6	Single crochet on the center of the ring

Legs of standing dog

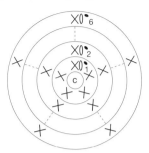

4 pieces

Row	No. of stitches	
6	5	No increase or decrease
5~3	5 each	
2	5	
1	5	Single crochet on the center of the ring

Tail

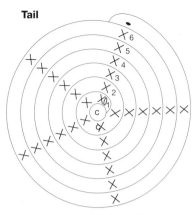

Row	No. of stitches	
6	5	No increase or decrease
5~3	5 each	
2	5	
1	5	Single crochet on the center of the ring

Mouth

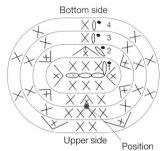

Bottom side

Upper side

Position of nose

Row	No. of stitches	
4	11	2 stitches decrease
3	13	No increase or decrease
2	13	3 stitches increase
1	10	Single crochet around 3 chain stitches

Ears

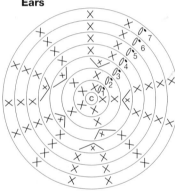

2 pieces

Row	No. of stitches	
7	12	No increase or decrease
6	12	
5	12	
4	12	2 stitches increase
3	10	5 stitches increase
2	5	No increase or decrease
1	5	Single crochet on the center of the ring

Position of parts

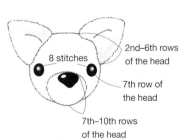

8 stitches

2nd–6th rows of the head

7th row of the head

7th–10th rows of the head

Seated dog

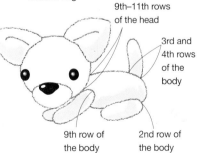

9th–11th rows of the head

3rd and 4th rows of the body

9th row of the body

2nd row of the body

Standing dog

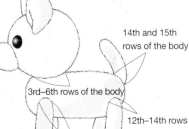

14th and 15th rows of the body

3rd–6th rows of the body

12th–14th rows of the body

3rd–5th rows of the body

Welsh Corgi See page 6.

The mouth is crocheted with white thread only, just like the Japanese Shiba. The tricolored dog's ears are crocheted like those of the Siberian Husky.

Materials

[Fawn]
Beige mohair thread, 0.35 oz
White mohair thread, 0.14 oz
Synthetic cotton
Black plastic sewing buttons, 2 pieces, 0.24 in
Brown nose, 1 piece, 0.47in

[Tricolor]
Black mohair thread, 0.35 oz
White mohair thread, 0.14 oz
Brown mohair thread, 0.11 oz
Synthetic cotton
Brown plastic eyes, 2 pieces, 0.35 in
Black nose, 1 piece, 0.47 in

Tool

Crochet hook, No. 4/0

Step-by-step method

[Fawn]
1. Sew each body part.
2. Stuff cotton inside the head and body.
3. Attach the eyes on the head.
4. Attach the nose on the mouth and stuff cotton in it.
5. Attach the mouth to the head by rolled darning.
6. Pass the remaining thread through the last row of the body and tie it tightly.
7. Pass the remaining thread through the last row of the head and tighten it lightly, then attach it to the body by rolled darning.
8. Attach the legs to the body by rolled darning.
9. Attach the ears to the head and the tail to the body by rolled darning.

[Tricolor]
Same as above. Attach the eyebrows after attaching the eyes in step 3.

Body c=center

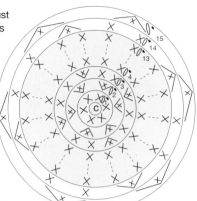

Row	No. of stitches	
15	6	6 stitches decrease
14	12	4 stitches decrease
13	16	No increase or decrease
12~5	16 each	
4	16	
3	16	4 stitches increase
2	12	6 stitches increase
1	6	Single crochet on the ring

☐ White

☐ Beige or black

Fawn dog's ears

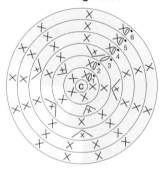

2 pieces

Row	No. of stitches	
6	12	No increase or decrease
5	12	
4	12	2 stitches increase
3	10	3 stitches increase
2	7	2 stitches increase
1	5	Single crochet on the ring

☐ Beige   ☐ White

Legs

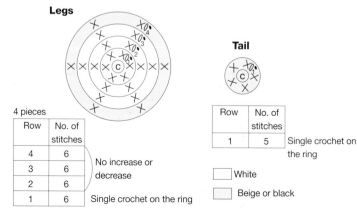

Tail

4 pieces

Row	No. of stitches	
4	6	No increase or decrease
3	6	
2	6	
1	6	Single crochet on the ring

Row	No. of stitches	
1	5	Single crochet on the ring

☐ White

☐ Beige or black

Head

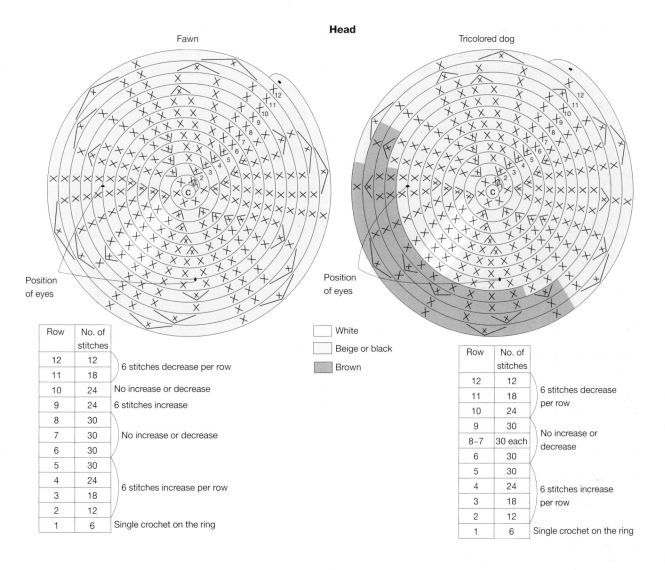

Fawn

Tricolored dog

Position of eyes

Position of eyes

	White
	Beige or black
	Brown

Row	No. of stitches	
12	12	6 stitches decrease per row
11	18	
10	24	No increase or decrease
9	24	6 stitches increase
8	30	No increase or decrease
7	30	
6	30	
5	30	6 stitches increase per row
4	24	
3	18	
2	12	
1	6	Single crochet on the ring

Row	No. of stitches	
12	12	6 stitches decrease per row
11	18	
10	24	
9	30	No increase or decrease
8~7	30 each	
6	30	
5	30	6 stitches increase per row
4	24	
3	18	
2	12	
1	6	Single crochet on the ring

Position of body parts

For the tricolored dog, the brown part is embroidered on the 5th and 6th rows of the head.

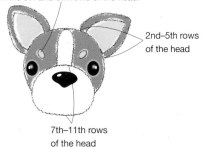

2nd–5th rows of the head

7th–11th rows of the head

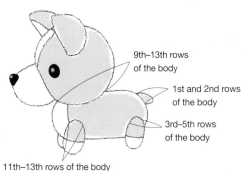

9th–13th rows of the body

1st and 2nd rows of the body

3rd–5th rows of the body

11th–13th rows of the body

Cavalier King Charles Spaniel See page 10.

The mouth and the Blenheim dog's legs are crocheted with white thread only, just like the Japanese Shiba. The tricolored dog's legs are knitted like those of a standing Chihuahua.

Materials

[Blenheim]
Brown thread, 0.46 oz
White thread, 0.71 oz
Synthetic cotton
Brown plastic eyes, 2 pieces, 0.35 in
Black nose, 1 piece, 0.47 in

[Tricolor]
White bulky thread, 0.42 oz
Black bulky thread, 0.49 oz
Brown bulky thread, 0.14 oz
Synthetic cotton
Brown plastic eyes, 2 pieces, 0.35 in
Black nose, 1 piece, 0.47 in

Tool

Crochet hook, No. 4/0

Step-by-step method

[Blenheim]
1. Sew each body part.
2. Stuff cotton inside the head, body, and legs.
3. Attach the eyes on the head.
4. Attach the nose on the mouth and stuff cotton in it.
5. Attach the mouth to the head by rolled darning.
6. Attach the body to the head by rolled darning.
7. Attach the legs and the tail to the body by rolled darning.
8. Make the ears by winding the thread around a sheet of cardboard.
9. Attach the ears to the head by rolled darning.

[Tricolor]
1–2. Same as above.
3. Attach the eyes and the eyebrows on the head.
4–5. Same as above.
6. Pass the remaining thread through the last row of the body and tie it tightly.
7. Pass the remaining thread through the last row of the head and tighten it lightly, then attach it to the body by rolled darning.
8. Attach the legs and the tail to the body by rolled darning, following the same steps for the ears.

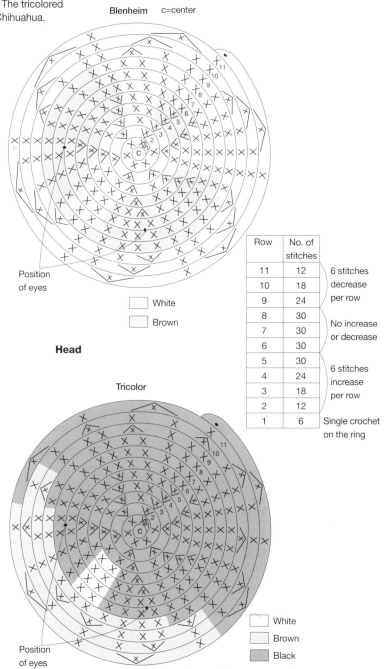

Blenheim   c=center

Position of eyes

☐ White
☐ Brown

Head

Tricolor

Position of eyes

☐ White
☐ Brown
■ Black

Row	No. of stitches	
11	12	6 stitches decrease per row
10	18	
9	24	
8	30	No increase or decrease
7	30	
6	30	
5	30	6 stitches increase per row
4	24	
3	18	
2	12	
1	6	Single crochet on the ring

Body

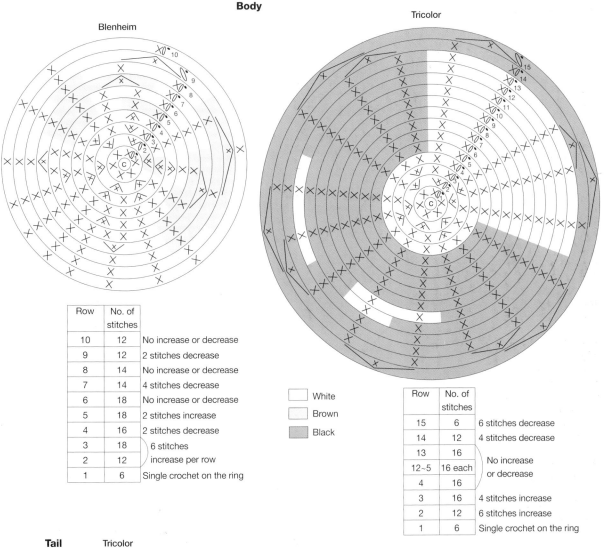

Blenheim

Tricolor

White	(white box)
Brown	(light box)
Black	(gray box)

Row	No. of stitches	
10	12	No increase or decrease
9	12	2 stitches decrease
8	14	No increase or decrease
7	14	4 stitches decrease
6	18	No increase or decrease
5	18	2 stitches increase
4	16	2 stitches decrease
3	18	6 stitches increase per row
2	12	
1	6	Single crochet on the ring

Row	No. of stitches	
15	6	6 stitches decrease
14	12	4 stitches decrease
13	16	No increase or decrease
12~5	16 each	
4	16	
3	16	4 stitches increase
2	12	6 stitches increase
1	6	Single crochet on the ring

Tail Tricolor

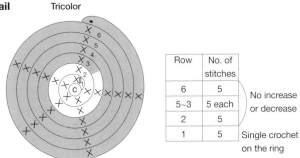

Row	No. of stitches	
6	5	No increase or decrease
5~3	5 each	
2	5	
1	5	Single crochet on the ring

For the Blenheim dog's tail, use white thread only.

Ears (2 pieces)

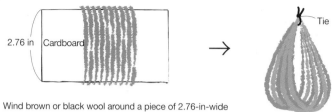

Wind brown or black wool around a piece of 2.76-in-wide cardboard ten times, then pull it out of the cardboard and tie the top with wool.

Position of body parts

Blenheim

4th row of the head (3 stitches away from the eye)

6th–10th rows of the head

9th row of the body

2nd–4th rows of the body

2nd–4th rows of the body

Tricolor

4th row of the head (3 stitches away from the eye)

Embroider with brown thread on the 4th and 5th rows of the head.

6th–10th rows of the head

3rd–5th rows of the body

14th and 15th rows of the body

12th–14th rows of the body

Labrador Retriever   See page 16.

The head and mouth are crocheted in the same way as those of the Miniature Dachshund. The black dog's body and legs are crocheted in the same way as the Japanese Shiba, and those for the yellow dog are crocheted like the standing Chihuahua. The tail is crocheted like the Chihuahua's, and the rest of the parts are crocheted with a single color.

Materials
[Yellow]
Beige thread, 0.42 oz
Synthetic cotton
Black plastic sewing buttons, 2 pieces, 0.24 in
Black nose, 1 piece, 0.47 in

[Black]
Black thread, 0.39 oz
Synthetic cotton
Brown plastic eyes, 2 pieces, 0.35 in
Black nose, 1 piece, 0.47 in

Tool
Crochet hook, No. 4/0

Step-by-step method
[Yellow]
1. Sew each body part.
2. Stuff cotton inside the head, body, and legs.
3. Attach the eyes on the head.
4. Attach the nose on the mouth and stuff cotton in it.
5. Attach the mouth to the head by rolled darning.
6. Pass the remaining thread through the last row of the body, and tie it tightly.
7. Pass the remaining thread through the last row of the head and tighten it lightly, then, attach it to the body by rolled darning.
8. Attach the legs to the body by rolled darning.
9. Fold the ears in half and sew each of them with the remaining thread.
10. Attach the ears to the head, and the tail to the body by rolled darning.

[Black]
1–5. Same as above
6. Attach the body to the head by rolled darning.
7–9. Follow steps 8–10.

Ears   c=center

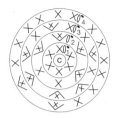

Row	No. of stitches	
4	14	2 stitches decrease
3	16	6 stitches increase
2	10	4 stitches increase
1	6	Single crochet on the ring

2 pieces

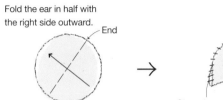

Fold the ear in half with the right side outward.

End

Center

Close the ear with the remaining thread.

Position of body parts

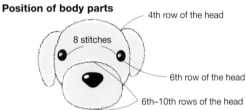

4th row of the head

8 stitches

6th row of the head

6th–10th rows of the head

Black

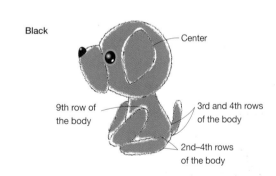

Center

9th row of the body

3rd and 4th rows of the body

2nd–4th rows of the body

Yellow

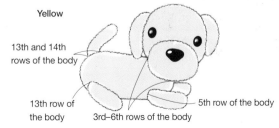

13th and 14th rows of the body

13th row of the body

3rd–6th rows of the body

5th row of the body

Miniature Dachshund   See page 12.

The cream dog is crocheted with a single color only. The red dog's ears and tail are knitted in different colors. The colors for the black and tan, and chocolate and cream dogs' mouths, toes, and eyebrows are altered.

Materials

[Red]
Brown thread, 0.35 oz
Chocolate-colored thread, 0.14 oz
[Black and Tan]
Black thread, 0.35 oz
Brown thread, 0.14 oz
[Cream]
Beige thread, 0.46 oz
[Chocolate and Cream]
Chocolate-colored thread, 0.35 oz
Beige thread, 0.14 oz
Synthetic cotton
[Red, Cream, Chocolate and Cream]
Black plastic sewing buttons, 2 pieces each, 0.24 in
[Black and Tan]
Brown plastic eyes, 2 pieces, 0.35 in
[Red, Cream, Chocolate and Cream]
Brown nose, 1 piece each, 0.47 in
[Black and Tan]
Black nose, 1 piece, 0.47 in

Tool

Crochet hook, No. 4/0

Step-by-step method (for all four types)

1. Sew each body part.
2. Stuff cotton inside the head, body, and legs.
3. Attach the eyes on the head. Attach the eyebrows for the black and tan, and chocolate and cream dogs.
4. Attach the nose on the mouth, and stuff cotton in it.
5. Attach the mouth to the head by rolled darning.
6. Pass the remaining thread through the last row of the body, and tie it tightly.
7. Pass the remaining thread through the last row of the head, and tighten it lightly, then, attach it to the body by rolled darning.
8. Attach the legs to the body by rolled darning.
9. Fold the ears in half, and sew each of them with the remaining thread.
10. Attach the ears on the head and the tail to the body by rolled darning.

Mouth

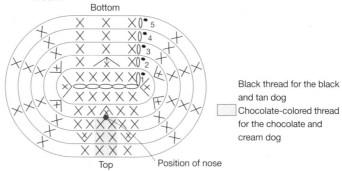

Black thread for the black and tan dog

Chocolate-colored thread for the chocolate and cream dog

Position of nose

Row	No. of stitches	
5	15	No increase or decrease
4	15	2 stitches decrease
3	17	No increase or decrease
2	17	3 stitches increase
1	14	Single crochet on five chain stitches

Body   c=center

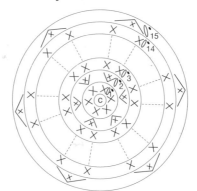

Row	No. of stitches	
15	6	6 stitches decrease
14	12	No increase or decrease
13~4	12 each	
3	12	
2	12	6 stitches increase
1	6	Single crochet on the ring

Ears

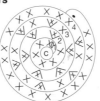

2 pieces

Row	No. of stitches	
4	18	No increase or decrease
3	18	6 stitches increase per row
2	12	
1	6	Single crochet on the ring

(See page 53 for the step-by-step method of the ears.)

Tail

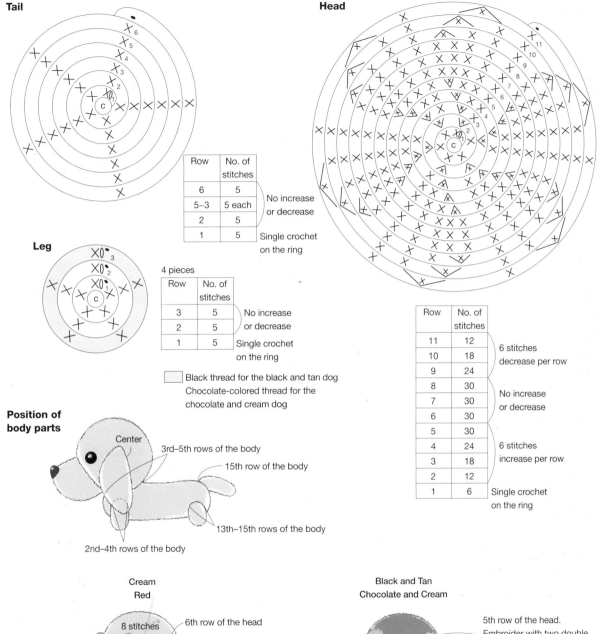

Row	No. of stitches	
6	5	No increase or decrease
5~3	5 each	
2	5	
1	5	Single crochet on the ring

Head

Leg

4 pieces

Row	No. of stitches	
3	5	No increase or decrease
2	5	
1	5	Single crochet on the ring

Black thread for the black and tan dog
Chocolate-colored thread for the chocolate and cream dog

Row	No. of stitches	
11	12	6 stitches decrease per row
10	18	
9	24	
8	30	No increase or decrease
7	30	
6	30	
5	30	
4	24	6 stitches increase per row
3	18	
2	12	
1	6	Single crochet on the ring

Position of body parts

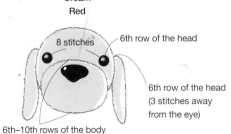

Center
3rd–5th rows of the body
15th row of the body
13th–15th rows of the body
2nd–4th rows of the body

Cream
Red

8 stitches
6th row of the head
6th row of the head (3 stitches away from the eye)
6th–10th rows of the body

Black and Tan
Chocolate and Cream

5th row of the head.
Embroider with two double crochets above the eyes with the thread of the same color as the toes.
The other parts are crocheted in the same way as the cream dog.

Siberian Husky See page 14.

The mouth, tail, and the gray dog's body are crocheted in the same way as those of the Japanese Shiba. The mouth is crocheted with white thread only.

Materials

[Gray]
Gray bulky thread, 0.46 oz
White bulky thread, 0.46 oz

[Black]
Black bulky thread, 0.6 oz
White bulky thread, 0.46 oz

Synthetic cotton
Blue plastic eyes, 2 pairs, 0.35 in
Black nose, 1 pair, 0.47 in

Tool

Crochet hook, No. 4/0

Step-by-step method

[Gray]
1. Sew each body part.
2. Stuff cotton inside the head, body, and legs.
3. Attach the eyes on the head, and embroider a line in the forehead.
4. Attach the nose on the mouth, and stuff cotton in it.
5. Attach the mouth to the head by rolled darning.
6. Attach the body to the head by rolled darning.
7. Attach the legs to the body by rolled darning.
8. Attach the ears on the head, and the tail to the body by rolled darning.

[Black]
1–5. Same as above
6. Pass the remaining thread through the last row of the body and tie it tightly.
7. Pass the remaining thread through the last row of the head and tighten it lightly, then, attach it to the body by rolled darning.
8. Attach the legs to the body by rolled darning.
9. Attach the ears on the head, and the tail to the body by rolled darning.

Head c=center

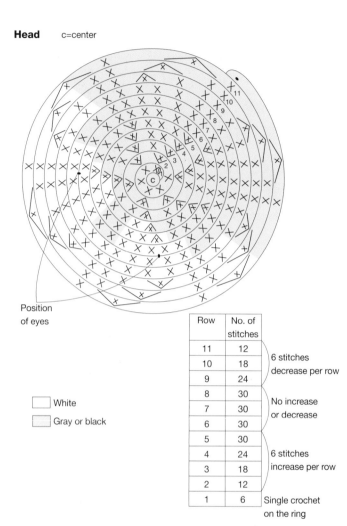

Position of eyes

☐ White
▨ Gray or black

Row	No. of stitches	
11	12	6 stitches decrease per row
10	18	
9	24	
8	30	No increase or decrease
7	30	
6	30	
5	30	
4	24	6 stitches increase per row
3	18	
2	12	
1	6	Single crochet on the ring

Ears

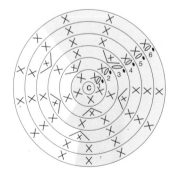

2 pieces

Row	No. of stitches	
6	12	No increase or decrease
5	12	
4	12	2 stitches increase
3	10	3 stitches increase
2	7	2 stitches increase
1	5	Single crochet on the ring

Black dog's body

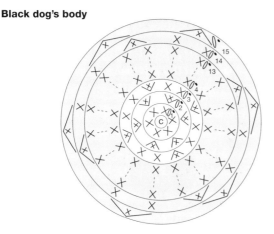

Row	No. of stitches	
15	6	6 stitches decrease
14	12	4 stitches decrease
13	16	
12~5	16	No increase or decrease
4	16	
3	16	4 stitches increase
2	12	6 stitches increase
1	6	Single crochet on the ring

Legs

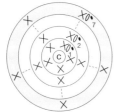

Gray dog's front legs, 2 pieces

Row	No. of stitches	
7	5	
6~3	5	No increase or decrease
2	5	
1	5	Single crochet on the ring

7th row: gray

Gray dog's hind legs, 2 pieces; Black dog's legs, 4 pieces

Row	No. of stitches	
6	5	
5~3	5	No increase or decrease
2	5	
1	5	Single crochet on the ring

7th row: gray or black

Position of body parts

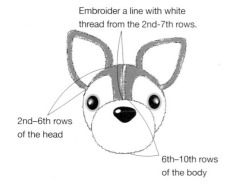

Embroider a line with white thread from the 2nd-7th rows.

2nd–6th rows of the head

6th–10th rows of the body

Black

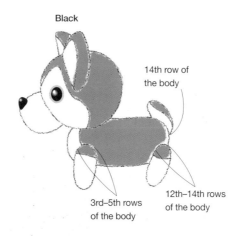

14th row of the body

3rd–5th rows of the body

12th–14th rows of the body

Gray

9th row of the body

2nd row of the body

2nd–4th rows of the body

Mother Beagle See page 24.

The mouth and ears are crocheted in the same way as those of the Miniature Dachshund. The mouth is crocheted with white thread, and the ears are crocheted with brown thread.

Materials
Brown thread, 0.35 oz
White thread, 0.18 oz
Black thread, 0.11 oz
Synthetic cotton
Black plastic sewing buttons, 2 pieces, 0.24 in
Black nose, 1 piece, 0.47 in

Tool
Crochet hook, No. 4/0

Step-by-step method
1. Sew each body part.
2. Stuff cotton inside the head, body, and legs.
3. Attach the eyes on the head.
4. Attach the nose on the mouth, and stuff cotton in it.
5. Attach the mouth to the head by rolled darning.
6. Attach the body to the head by rolled darning.
7. Attach the legs to the body by rolled darning.
8. Fold the ears in half, and sew each of them with the remaining thread.
9. Attach the ears to the head, and the tail to the body by rolled darning.

Head c=center

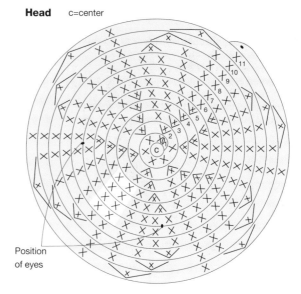

Position of eyes

☐ White
☐ Brown

Row	No. of stitches	
11	12	6 stitches decrease per row
10	18	
9	24	
8	30	No increase or decrease
7	30	
6	30	
5	30	
4	24	6 stitches increase per row
3	18	
2	12	
1	6	Single crochet on the ring

Legs

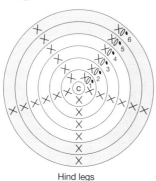

Hind legs

Front legs, 2 pieces
Crochet the 1st to 5th rows with white thread, and the 6th to 7th rows with brown thread.

Row	No. of stitches	
7	5	No increase or decrease
6~3	5 each	
2	5	
1	5	Single crochet on the ring

Hind legs, 2 pieces

Row	No. of stitches	
6	5	No increase or decrease
5~3	5 each	
2	5	
1	5	Single crochet on the ring

60

Body

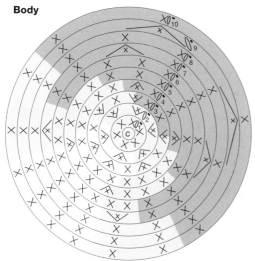

Tail

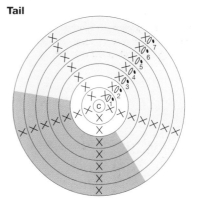

Row	No. of stitches	
7	5	No increase or decrease
6~3	5 each	
2	5	
1	5	Single crochet on the ring

☐ White

☐ Brown

▨ Black

Row	No. of stitches	
10	12	No increase or decrease
9	12	2 stitches decrease
8	14	No increase or decrease
7	14	4 stitches decrease
6	18	No increase or decrease
5	18	2 stitches increase
4	16	2 stitches decrease
3	18	6 stitches increase per row
2	12	
1	6	Single crochet on the ring

Position of body parts

6th row of the head (3 stitches away from the eye)

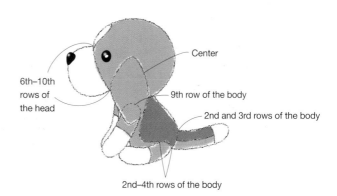

6th–10th rows of the head

Center

9th row of the body

2nd and 3rd rows of the body

2nd–4th rows of the body

Miniature Schnauzer   See page 20.

The body is crocheted with black or gray thread, just like the standing Chihuahua.

Materials

[Salt and pepper]
Gray bulky thread, 0.71 oz
White bulky thread, 0.28 oz

[Black and white]
Black bulky thread, 0.71 oz
White bulky thread, 0.28 oz

Synthetic cotton
Black plastic sewing buttons, 2 pairs, 0.24 in
Black nose, 1 pair, 0.47 in

Tool

Crochet hook, No. 4/0

Step-by-step method

1. Sew each body part.
2. Stuff cotton inside the head, body, and legs.
3. Attach the eyes and the eyebrows on the head.
4. Attach the nose on the mouth and stuff cotton in it.
5. Attach the mouth on the head by rolled darning.
6. Pass the remaining thread through the last row of the body, and tie it tightly.
7. Pass the remaining thread through the last row of the head, and tighten it lightly, then, attach it to the body by rolled darning.
8. Attach the legs to the body by rolled darning.
9. Attach the ears to the head and the tail to the body by rolled darning.
10. Sew and glue the moustache on the mouth, and trim the ends of the moustache.

Head   c=center

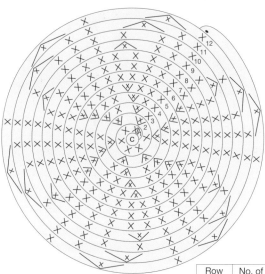

☐ White
☐ Black or gray

Row	No. of stitches	
12	12	6 stitches decrease per row
11	18	
10	24	No increase or decrease
9	24	6 stitches decrease
8	30	No increase or decrease
7	30	
6	30	
5	30	6 stitches increase per row
4	24	
3	18	
2	12	
1	6	Single crochet on the ring

Mouth   Bottom

Row	No. of stitches	
6	15	No increase or decrease
5	15	
4	15	2 stitches decrease
3	17	No increase or decrease
2	17	3 stitches increase
1	14	Single crochet on 5 chain stitches

Top   Position of nose

Ears

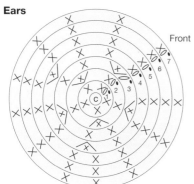

Front

Legs

Tail

Row	No. of stitches	
2	5	No increase or decrease
1	5	Single crochet on the ring

☐ White

☐ Black or gray

2 pieces

Row	No. of stitches	
7	12	No increase or decrease
6	12	
5	12	
4	12	2 stitches increase
3	10	3 stitches increase
2	7	2 stitches increase
1	5	Single crochet on the ring

4 pieces

Row	No. of stitches	
7	6	No increase or decrease
6~3	6 each	
2	6	
1	6	Single crochet on the ring

Position of body parts

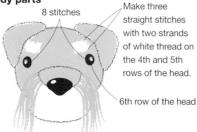

8 stitches

Make three straight stitches with two strands of white thread on the 4th and 5th rows of the head.

6th row of the head

Black and silver

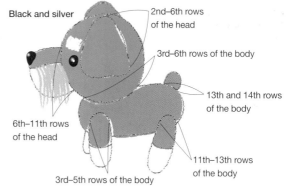

2nd–6th rows of the head

3rd–6th rows of the body

13th and 14th rows of the body

11th–13th rows of the body

6th–11th rows of the head

3rd–5th rows of the body

Attaching the moustache

❶ Pass a strand of wool across the border and tie.

❷ Glue the thread

❸ Trim and arrange the ends of the moustache.

Salt and pepper

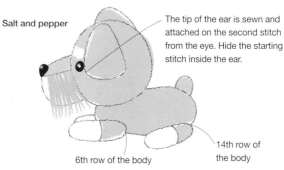

The tip of the ear is sewn and attached on the second stitch from the eye. Hide the starting stitch inside the ear.

6th row of the body

14th row of the body

French Bulldog   See page 22.

The mouth, legs, and body of the seated dog are crocheted with white thread, just like the Japanese Shiba, and the four legs of the reclining dog are crocheted as many as six rows. The tail is crocheted in the same way as the Welsh Corgi.

Materials

White thread, 0.42 oz
Black thread, 0.14 oz
Pink thread, 0.11 oz
Synthetic cotton
Transparent plastic eyes, 2 pairs, 0.35 in
Black nose, 1 pair, 0.47 in

Tool

Crochet hook, No. 4/0

Step-by-step method

[Seated dog]
1. Sew each body part.
2. Stuff cotton inside the head, body, and legs.
3. Attach the eyes on the head. Paint the reverse side of the eyes with a correction fluid.
4. Attach the nose on the mouth with its seam in front, and stuff cotton in it.
5. Attach the mouth to the head by rolled darning.
6. Attach the body to the head by rolled darning.
7. Attach the legs to the body by rolled darning.
8. Attach the ears on the head and the tail to the body by rolled darning.

[Reclining dog]
1–5. Same as above.
6. Pass the remaining thread through the last row of the body, and tie it tightly.
7. Pass the remaining thread through the last row of the head, and tighten it lightly, then, attach it to the body by rolled darning.
8. Attach the legs to the body by rolled darning.
9. Attach the ears to the head, and the tail to the body by rolled darning.

For both types of dogs, sew about three stitches on the first row with black thread.

Head   c=center

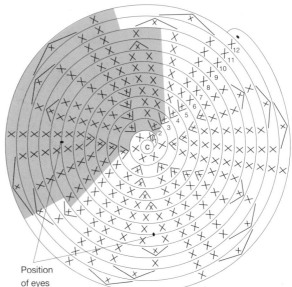

Position of eyes

Row	No. of stitches	
12	12	6 stitches decrease per row
11	18	
10	24	No increase or decrease
9	24	6 stitches decrease
8	30	No increase or decrease
7	30	
6	30	
5	30	6 stitches increase per row
4	24	
3	18	
2	12	
1	6	Single crochet on the ring

Position of body parts

3rd–6th rows of the head

Reclining body of the French Bulldog

15
14
13
12
11
10
9
8
7
6
5
4
3
2

	White
	Pink
	Black

Row	No. of stitches	
15	6	6 stitches decrease
14	12	4 stitches decrease
13	16	No increase or decrease
12~5	16 each	
4	16	
3	16	4 stitches increase
2	12	6 stitches increase
1	6	Single crochet on the ring

Ears

Right ear

6
5
4
3
2

Left ear

6
5
4
3
2
1

Row	No. of stitches	
6	12	No increase or decrease
5	12	
4	12	2 stitches increase
3	10	3 stitches increase
2	7	2 stitches increase
1	5	Single crochet on the ring

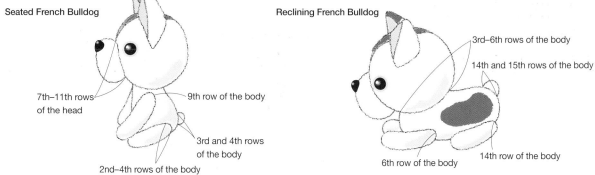

Seated French Bulldog

7th–11th rows of the head

9th row of the body

3rd and 4th rows of the body

2nd–4th rows of the body

Reclining French Bulldog

3rd–6th rows of the body

14th and 15th rows of the body

6th row of the body

14th row of the body

Pug See page 26.

The body and legs of the standing dog are crocheted just like the Chihuahua. The legs of the seated dog are crocheted with a single color, just like the Japanese Shiba. The black pug is crocheted with black thread.

Materials

[Seated black]
Black thread, 0.42 oz
Synthetic cotton
Brown plastic eyes, 2 pieces, 0.35 in
Black nose, 1 piece, 0.47 in

[Seated fawn]
Beige thread, 0.32 oz
Black thread, 0.18 oz
(For the eyes and nose, same as the seated black dog.)

[Standing black]
Black thread, 0.46 oz
Transparent plastic eyes, 2 pieces, 0.35 in
(For the nose, same as the seated black dog.)

[Standing fawn]
Beige thread, 0.35 oz
Black thread, 0.18 oz
Transparent plastic eyes, 2 pieces, 0.35 in
(For the nose, same as the seated black dog.)

Tool

Crochet hook, No. 4/0

Step-by-step method

[Seated dog]
1. Sew each body part.
2. Stuff cotton inside the head, body, and legs.
3. Attach the eyes on the head. (For the white of the eyes, paint the reverse side of the eyes with correction fluid.)
4. Attach the nose on the mouth, and stuff cotton in it.
5. Attach the mouth to the head by rolled darning.
6. Attach the body to the head by rolled darning.
7. Attach the legs to the body by rolled darning.
8. Attach the ears to the head, and the tail to the body by rolled darning.

[Standing dog]
1–5. Same as above.
6. Pass the remaining thread through the last row of the body, and tie it tightly.
7. Pass the remaining thread through the last row of the head and tighten it lightly, then, attach it to the body by rolled darning.
8. Attach the legs and the tail to the body by rolled darning.
9. Attach the ears to the head by rolled darning.

Head c=center

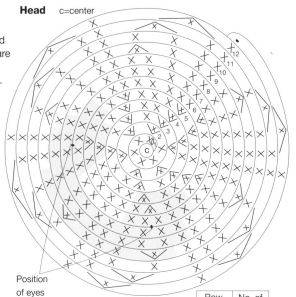

Position of eyes

☐ Beige
☐ Black

Row	No. of stitches	
12	12	6 stitches
11	18	decrease per row
10	24	No increase or decrease
9	24	6 stitches decrease
8	30	No increase
7	30	or decrease
6	30	
5	30	
4	24	6 stitches increase
3	18	per row
2	12	
1	6	Single crochet on the ring

Mouth Bottom

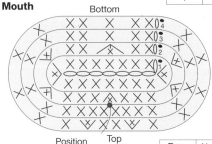

Position of nose Top

Row	No. of stitches	
4	19	2 stitches decrease
3	21	No increase or decrease
2	21	3 stitches increase
1	18	Single crochet on 7 chain stitches

Body of Seated Pug

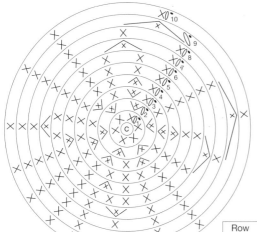

Ears

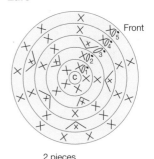

Front

2 pieces

Row	No. of stitches	
5	12	No increase or decrease
4	12	2 stitches increase
3	10	3 stitches increase
2	7	2 stitches increase
1	5	Single crochet on the ring

Tail

X X X X X X ⟩ ←1

Single row: Sew six stitches with a single crochet on six starting chains.

Row	No. of stitches	
10	12	No increase or decrease
9	12	2 stitches decrease
8	14	No increase or decrease
7	14	4 stitches decrease
6	18	No increase or decrease
5	18	2 stitches increase
4	16	2 stitches decrease
3	18	6 stitches increase per row
2	12	
1	6	Single crochet on the ring

Position of body parts

Seated Pug

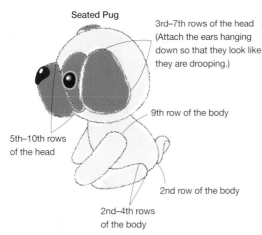

3rd–7th rows of the head (Attach the ears hanging down so that they look like they are drooping.)

9th row of the body

5th–10th rows of the head

2nd row of the body

2nd–4th rows of the body

Standing Pug

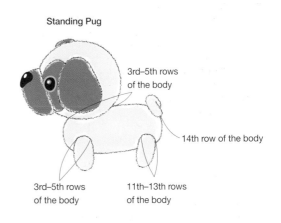

3rd–5th rows of the body

14th row of the body

3rd–5th rows of the body

11th–13th rows of the body

Cellular Phone Accessories   See page 28.

Materials

Synthetic cotton
Double round ring, 1 piece, 0.19 in.
 in diameter
Strap with a lobster claw clasp

Large Miniature Schnauzer
Gray light thread, 0.25 oz
White light thread, 0.39 oz
Red thread, some
Black eyes, 2 pieces, 0.15 in
Black nose, 1 piece, 0.35 in

Chihuahua
White thread, 0.14 oz
Red thread, some
Black eyes, 2 pieces, 0.16 in
Black nose, 1 piece, 0.18 in

Miniature Dachshund

[Red]
Beige thread, 0.11 oz
Chocolate-colored thread, 0.07 oz
Red thread, some

[Chocolate and Cream]
Chocolate-colored thread, 0.11 oz
Beige thread, 0.07 oz
Red thread, some

[Black and Tan]
Black thread, 0.11 oz
Beige thread, 0.07 oz
Red thread, some

[Red, Chocolate and Cream]
Black eyes, 2 pieces, 0.12 in

[Black and Tan]
Brown plastic eyes, 2 pieces, 0.18 in

[Red, Chocolate and Cream]
Brown nose, 1 piece, 0.18 in

[Black and Tan]
Black nose, 1 piece, 0.18 in

Small Miniature Schnauzer
Gray thread, 0.11 oz
White thread, 0.07 oz
Red thread, some
Black eyes, 2 pieces, 0.12 in
Black nose, 1 piece, 0.18 in

Pug
Beige thread, 0.28 oz
Black thread, 0.28 oz
Red thread, some
Brown plastic eyes, 2 pieces,
0.24 in
Black nose, 1 piece, 0.35 in

Beagle
Brown light thread, 0.21 oz
White light thread, 0.11 oz
Black light thread, 0.11 oz
Red thread, some
Black eyes, 2 pieces, 0.15 in
Black nose, 1 piece, 0.35 in

Japanese Shiba
Brown light thread, 0.21 oz
White light thread, 0.14 oz
Red thread, some
Black eyes, 2 pieces, 0.15 in
Black nose, 1 piece, 0.35 in

Welsh Corgi
White thread, 0.11 oz
Beige thread, 0.25 oz
Red thread, some
Black eyes, 2 pieces, 0.15 in
Brown nose, 1 piece, 0.35 in

Tools

Large Miniature Schnauzer, Pug, Beagle, Japanese Shiba, Welsh Corgi
Crochet hook, No. 3/0
Crochet hook No. 2/0 (to knit the collar)

Chihuahua, Miniature Dachshund, Small Miniature Schnauzer
Lacing needle, No.2

Step-by-step method

1. Sew each body part. To make the head, see the corresponding diagrams for each dog.
2. Stuff cotton inside the body (except for the legs).
3. Attach the body to the head by rolled darning.
4. Attach the legs and tail to the body by rolled darning.
5. Attach the ears to the head by rolled darning.
6. Make the collar by sewing chain stitches in proportion to the neck circumference, then wind it around the neck, and stitch it up.
7. Sew a double round ring on the head, and attach the strap.

Body

c=center

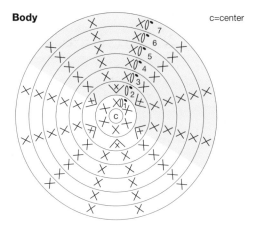

Row	No. of stitches	
7	12	No increase or decrease
6~4	12 each	
3	12	
2	12	6 stitches increase
1	6	Single crochet on the ring

Use the same color of the head for the Beagle only.

Black for the Beagle. Use a single color for the other dogs.

Legs

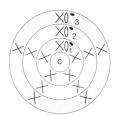

4 pieces

Row	No. of stitches	
3	5	No increase
2	5	or decrease
1	5	Single crochet on the ring

White or beige

Same color for the body
Use a single color for the Pug, Chihuahua, and red Miniature Dachshund, and two colors for the other dogs.

Tail

Miniature Dachshund, Chihuahua, Beagle

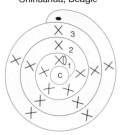

Row	No. of stitches	
3	5	No increase
2	5	or decrease
1	5	Single crochet on the ring

White for the Beagle

Black for the Beagle
Use a single color for the other dogs.

6 single crochet stitches on the ring

(See page 33 for the **Japanese Shiba**.)
(See page 67 for the **Pug**.)
(See page 63 for the **Miniature Schnauzer**.)

Position of body parts

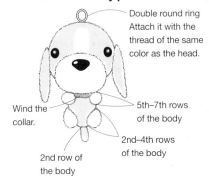

Double round ring
Attach it with the thread of the same color as the head.

Wind the collar.

2nd row of the body

5th–7th rows of the body

2nd–4th rows of the body

Dog bowl, Dog food   See page 1.

Materials

[Dog bowl]
Red thread, 0.11 oz

[Dog food]
White thread, 0.07 oz

Synthetic cotton

Tool

[Dog bowl]
Crochet hook, No. 4/0

[Dog food]
Crochet hook, No. 3/0

Dog bowl

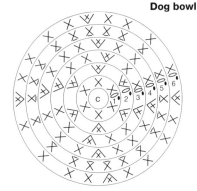

Row	No. of stitches	
6	24	4 stitches increase
5	20	Ridge stitches with no increase or decrease
4	20	4 stitches increase
3	16	per row
2	12	6 stitches increase
1	6	Single crochet on the ring

Dog food

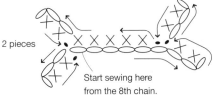

2 pieces

Start sewing here from the 8th chain.

Sew two pieces together by making the front side of each piece face inward, and the reverse sides of both pieces face outward, then stitch them together while stuffing cotton inside.

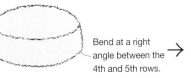

Bend at a right angle between the 4th and 5th rows.

Press down the part in the 1st through 4th rows from the top, denting it.

Mitsuki Hoshi

In 1999, Mitsuki, who likes Mickey Mouse very much, bought a Mickey Mouse knitting kit, and that occasion became the start of her self-taught Amigurumi lessons. In the same year, her friend showed her a book written by an Amigurumi creator, which impressed her so much, that she pursued the goal of becoming an Amigurumi creator herself, to making everything from food to animals, and abiding by the motto "create everything with wool."

In 2002, she launched her Web site, which presents purely Amigurumi dogs. Eventually, she devoted herself entirely to the creation of Amigurumi dogs. Her works have frequently been presented in pet magazines. Currently, she also teaches a class in crocheting Amigurumi dogs.

http://hoshi-mitsuki.com/